Mythological Creatures of Canada: Exploring the Rich Tapestry of Folklore and Legend

By: Rinn Skyborn

Canada, with its vast landscapes and diverse cultures, boasts a rich tapestry of folklore and mythology. Among the intriguing elements of Canadian folklore are its mythical creatures – beings that have captured the imagination of generations.

From the majestic forests of British Columbia to the icy waters of the Arctic, these creatures are deeply ingrained in the cultural heritage of the nation. In this Novel, we will embark on a journey to explore some of the most fascinating mythological creatures of Canada, delving into their origins, characteristics, and significance within Canadian folklore.

Table of contents

- Description and Behavior

- Cultural Significance and Beliefs

- Qallupilluit in Contemporary Context

Loup Garou: Shape Shifting Werewolves of French-Canadian Folklore

- Origins and Evolution of the Legend

- Characteristics and Behavior

- Cultural influence and Beliefs

- Modern Interpretations and Adaptations

Memegwesi: Mischievous Spirits of Algonquian Mythology

- Algonquian Traditions and Stories

- Descriptions and Attributes

- Role in Folklore and Everyday Life

- Memegwesi in Indigenous Revival Movements

Introduction to the Wendigo: A Chilling Legend of the North

The Wendigo

Deep within the frigid wilderness of Canada's northern reaches lies a tale as chilling as the icy winds that sweep across the tundra. It is a legend whispered in hushed tones around camp fires and shared in solemn tones among indigenous and settlers alive; This is the Legend of the Wendigo.

The Wendigo is a creature steeped in the folklore of various Indigenous cultures across Northern America, including the Algonquian, Ojibwe, Cree, and Inuit peoples. Its name alone is enough to send tremors down your spine, evoking images of a monstrous being lurking in the shadows, hungry for human flesh.

However, the Wendigo is more than just a creature of myth and legend; it is a powerful symbol embodying the darkest aspects of human nature and the harsh realities of survival in the darkest aspects of the human nature and harsh realities of survival in the unforgiving wilderness.

Described as a malevolent spirit or cannibalistic monster, the Wendigo is said to possess those who succumb to greed, hunger, or desperation, driving them to commit unspeakable acts of violence and depravity.

In this introduction to Wendigo, we will delve into the origins, characteristics, and cultural significance of this enigmatic creature. From its ancient roots in indigenous oral traditions to its enduring presence in contemporary literature, film and popular culture, the Wendigo continues to haunt the collective imagination, serving as a cautionary tale of the dangers that lurk in the darkness within us and the wilderness surrounding us.

Join us as us as we journey into the heart of darkness and uncover the chilling legend of the Wendigo, a creature that has haunted the North American wilderness for centuries.

Legends of a time when a great famine swept through the land, driving desperate souls to commit unspeakable acts, often driven to the brink of madness by hunger and despair.

However, the most chilling aspect of Wendigo was the ability to prey upon the weakness of humans, it whispers promises of power, wealth, and other riches, luring unsuspecting victims into its clutches with honeyed words and false promises. Then, at their most vulnerable the Wendigo is known to strike without mercy, consuming their flesh and leaving behind only a hollow shell of what once was.

The Wendigo is a legendary creature that originates from the folklore of various Indigenous people in Canada, particularly among the Algonquian-speaking tribes such as the Ojibwe, and Cree.

The legend of Wendigo remains a cautionary tale and is often depicted as a malevolent supernatural being associated with cannibalism, greed, and the harsh winter wilderness. Its origins and cultural significance are deeply rooted in many traditions and beliefs. The Wendigo remains a compelling and multifaceted figure of indigenous resilience, cultural heritage, and supernatural intrigue. Its presence is a legend that continues to captivate generations to come.

The Wendigo is continually portrayed as a sinister, otherworldly entity linked to violence, cannibalism, insatiable greed and the unforgiving depts of the winter wilds; Here are the description and characteristics commonly associated with the wendigo:

- Appearance:
  Physical appearances of Wendigo vary across different traditions, interpretations, and stories. However, it is often described as a tall, emaciated figure with elongated libs, twisted, contorted and gaunt skeletal frame; its flesh stretched and touched over bones as sharp as daggers. giving it a skeletal appearance. The Wendigo's eyes are often described as glowing or reflective, that pierce the darkness and it may have long, sharp claws like icy talons adorning its hands and teeth ready to tear apart any who cross its path.

- Size:
  The wendigo is typically depicted throughout many stories as towering over ordinary humans, emphasizing its supernatural nature and intimidating presence. In some legends, it is said to grow with each victim it consumes, becoming larger and more monstrous over time. -on average most sources state the Wendigo can be anywhere between 5-10 meters tall, even more.

- Cannibalistic Nature:

  The most defining characteristic of the Wendigo is its insatiable hunger for human flesh. According to legend, Wendigo is created when a person resorts to cannibalism changing them in ornate and unchangeable ways – mostly during times of famine or extreme hardship. By consuming human flesh, the individual becomes possessed by the spirit of the Wendigo, transforming them into a creature driven by an unending craving for flesh and blood.

- Cold and Winter:

  Wendigo are often associated with the cold and harsh winter wilderness of the northern regions where it is rumored to roam. It is believed to thrive in icy, desolate landscapes, emerging during times where individuals feel the most vulnerable in the wilderness.

- Supernatural Abilities:

  In addition to its physical prowess, the Wendigo is often attributed with its abilities such as stealth speed and the ability to control the weather in certain situations. It is said to possess powers of manipulation and deception, luring unsuspecting victims into its grasp.

- **Fear and Terror:**

  The Wendigo instills fear and terror without fail in those who have the unfortunate luck to encounter it, bother through its grotesque appearance and its reputation as a remorseless predator. It is often depicted as a malevolent force that prays on humans, particularly those who have strayed from traditional values or those who remain selfish and greedy.

Its appearance and characteristics may vary across different traditions, but its status as a fearsome and formidable creature remains consistent throughout folklore in Canada. The interpretation and symbolism of the Wendigo in Canada are complex, and deeply rooted in many different cultures and beliefs.

Here are several key interpretations and symbolic representations of the Wendigo:

- Moral Allegory:

  The Wendigo serves as a moral allegory, warning against the dangers of greed, selfishness, and the violation of moral values. The legend teaches that indulging in acts of cannibalism or unchecked consumption can lead to spiritual corruption and monstrous transformation. It emphasizes the importance of respect for nature, sharing resources, and maintaining harmony within our communities.

- Environmental Destruction:

  Wendigo are often interpreted as a symbol of environmental destruction and imbalance. Its association with the harsh winter wilderness and insatiable hunger mirrors humanity's exploitation of natural resources and disregard for the delicate balance of ecosystems; highlighting the consequences of greed and continual exploitation of the natural world.

- Colonialism and Cultural Disruption:
In some explanations, the Wendigo tends to focus on its symbolism of the destructive impact colonialism had and cultural disruption on Indigenous communities. The arrival of European settlers brought disease, displacement, and cultural assimilation, leading to social upheaval and loss of traditional ways of life. The wendigo legend may be seen as a metaphor for the erosion of the Indigenous identity and the struggle to maintain cultural resilience in the face of external pressures.

- Psychological and Spiritual Themes:
The Wendigo can also be interpreted on a psychological and spiritual level, representing our inner demons, primal instincts, and the darker aspects of human nature. It symbolizes the struggle between good and evil, the temptation of forbidden desires, and the consequences of giving in to base instincts. The legend encourages introspection and self-awareness, urging individuals to confront their inner demons and strive for spiritual balance.

- Survival and Resilience:
Despite its terrifying reputation, the Wendigo also embodies themes

of survival and flexibility in the face of adversity. Indigenous communities have adapted the legend as a means of passing down survival skills, traditional knowledge, and cultural values from generation to generation. Wendigo serves as a reminder of the strength and resourcefulness needed to endure harsh environments and overcome challenges.

- Cultural Identity and Heritage:
  Finally, the Wendigo holds significant cultural and symbolic importance within Indigenous communities, representing a connection to ancestral traditions, storytelling, and spiritual beliefs. By preserving and sharing the legends of the Wendigo, Indigenous peoples affirm their cultural identity and heritage, fostering a sense of solidarity and resilience in the face of historical and ongoing challenges.

The Wendigo is a complex and layered symbol that encompasses a wide range of interpretations and meanings within the context of Canadian Indigenous culture. It reflects profound themes of morality, environmental stewardship, cultural resilience, and spiritual understanding making it a rich and enduring symbol of folklore and mythology.

The legend of the Wendigo continues to hold a significant place in contemporary Canadian culture, influencing literature, film, art, and popular media. Here are some ways in which the Wendigo may appear in contemporary culture in Canada:

- Literature:

  Canadian authors have drawn upon the Wendigo legend as a source of inspiration in their literary works for many years. For example, Canadian novelist Joseph Boyden's novel "Three Day Road" incorporates elements of indigenous mythology, including references to the Wendigo. Similarly, Canadian horror author Andrew Pyper explores the theme of the Wendigo in his novel "The Wildfire Season," weaving indigenous folklore with contemporary story telling.

- Film and Television:

  The Wendigo has also made appearances in film and television productions such as the Canadian horror film "Wendigo" (2001), directed by Larry Fessenden, draws upon the legend of the Wendigo to create a chilling tale of supernatural terror in the wilderness. Additionally, the Wendigo has been featured in episodes of television series "Supernatural" and Haven," further popularizing the legend among audiences.

- Visual Arts:

  Canadian artists have depicted the Wendigo in various forms of visual art, including paintings, sculptures, and multimedia installations. Indigenous artists have explored the symbolism of the Wendigo within the context of indigenous identity, spirituality, and cultural heritage. These artistic representations serve to preserve and celebrate folklore while also engaging with contemporary themes and issues.

- Indigenous Cultural Revival:

  Within Indigenous communities, there has been a resurgence of interest in traditional storytelling, including legends such as the Wendigo. Elders and knowledge keepers play a vital role in passing down these oral traditions to the younger generations, assisting to preserve Indigenous languages, cultural practices, and spiritual beliefs. The Wendigo continues to be a prominent figure in Indigenous storytelling and cultural expression, serving as a connection to the ancestral knowledge and wisdom.

- Popular Culture and Merchandise:

  The Wendigo has also permeated popular culture beyond Canada, appearing in video games, graphic novels, and merchandise. Its iconic imagery in addition to themes of horror and survival resonate with audiences worldwide, contributing to its enduring popularity in contemporary media.

Legends state there was a time when a great famine swept through the land, driving desperate souls to commit unspeakable acts. Among them was a long traveler, driven to the brink of madness by hunger and despair. In a moment of desperate folly, he succumbed to the forbidden temptation, feasting upon the flesh of its fellow man.

Form twisted and contorted; its flesh stretched taut over bones as sharp as daggers. Glowing eyes pierced the darkness, reflecting the cold light of the moon above. Long claws, like icy talons, adorned his skeletal hands, ready to tear at any who dared cross its path.

It was not only its physical form that inspired fear and dread among those who knew of its existence; the Wendigo possessed powers beyond mortal comprehension, weaving illusions and manipulating the very elements to ensnare its prey. Its mastery over the icy winds and biting cold made it a true terror of the winter wilderness, continuing to strike fear into the hearts of all those who venture too close.

Yet the most chilling aspect of Wendigo was its ability to prey upon the weakness of the human soul. It whispered promises of power and wealth, luring unsuspecting victims into its clutches with honeyed words and false promises. And when they were at their most vulnerable, it struck without mercy, consuming their flesh, and leaving behind a hollow of a shell of what once was.

Introduction to Ogopogo: Canada's Legendary Lake Monster

Nestled amidst the majestic beauty of British Columbia's Okanagan Valley lies a mystery as deep as the waters of its pristine lakes. Here, beneath the tranquil surface of Okanagan Lake, lurks a creature of legend, known to locals and visitors alike as Ogopogo.

Ogopogo is Canada's most famous lake monster, a cryptid whose origins trace back centuries in the oral traditions of the indigenous Syilx people and whose presence continues to captivate the imagination of modern-day adventurers and skeptics alike.

In this introduction to Ogopogo, we embark on a journey into the heart of Okanagan Valley to uncover the myths, sightings, and mysteries surrounding this elusive creature. From ancient legends passed down through generations to contemporary accounts and scientific investigations, Ogopogo's story weaves a tapestry of wonder and intrigue that stretches across time and culture.

Join us as we delve into the depths of Okanagan Lake, where the legend of Ogopogo awaits, ready to tantalize and terrify with takes of serpentine monsters, mysterious sightings, and the enduring quest to unravel the secrets of Canada's legendary lake monster.

Ogopogo: Mysterious Serpent of the Okanagan Lake

The legend of Ogopogo, the mysterious serpent of Okanagan Lake in British Columbia, Canada, has captivated imaginations for generations. Here's an overview of the legends and lore surrounding Ogopogo:

- Indigenous Origins:
  The legend of Ogopogo has its roots in the oral traditions of the indigenous peoples of the Okanagan region, particularly the Syilx (Okanagan) people. They have long told stories of a large serpent-like creature inhabiting the depths of Okanagan Lake. The creature was believed to possess supernatural powers and was regarded both with fear and reverence.

- Appearance and Characteristics:
  Descriptions of Ogopogo vary, but it is often depicted as a long, serpent-like creature with humps protruding from the water.

Witnesses have reported seeing a creature ranging from 40-50 feet in length, with dark, scaly skin and serpentine head. Some accounts describe it as having a horse-like head or other unusual features.

- Encounters and Sightings:
  Over the years, there have been numerous reported sightings of Ogopogo by locals and visitors alike. These sightings range from fleeting glimpses of a large, unidentified creature swimming in the lake to more detailed observations describing its size, shape, and movements. While many sightings can be attributed to natural phenomena or misidentifications, others remain unexplained, fueling the mystery surrounding Ogopogo.

- Cultural Significance:
  Ogopogo holds significant cultural significance for the people of the Okanagan region. It is celebrated in local folklore, art, and festivals, serving as a symbol of the area's natural beauty and mystique. The legend of Ogopogo also attracts tourists to the Okanagan Valley, contributing to the region's economy and cultural identity.

- Scientific Interest:
  Despite the lack of conclusive evidence, Ogopogo has attracted the attention of cryptozoologists, scientists and enthusiasts interested in

unknown or undiscovered species. Expeditions and research efforts have been undertaken to investigate the phenomenon and search for evidence of Ogopogo's existence, including sonar surveys of Okanagan Lake and underwater exploration.

- Popular Culture:
Ogopogo has become an iconic figure in Canadian popular culture, appearing in books, film, television shows and other media. It has also been featured in documentaries exploring cryptozoology and aquatic mysteries, as well as in fictional works inspired by legend.

The legend of Ogopogo continues to intrigue and inspire wonder, sparking curiosity about the mysteries of the natural world and the enduring power of folklore and myth. Whether regarded as a mythical creature of legend or a real-life enigma waiting to be discovered, Ogopogo remains an enduring symbol of the Okanagan region's rich cultural heritage and beauty.

Descriptions and sightings of Ogopogo, the mysterious serpent of Okanagan Lake, vary widely, but they typically share common characteristics and themes.

Here are some examples of descriptions and reported sightings of Ogopogo:

- Long Serpentine Body:

  Many eyewitness accounts describe Ogopogo as having a long, serpent-like body, often compared to that of a giant snake or sea serpent. Witnesses report seeing a creature with multiple humps or coils protruding from the water, suggesting a large and elongated form.

- Large Size:

  Ogopogo is commonly described as a being of considerable size, with estimates ranging from 40 to 50 feet in length or even longer. Some witnesses claim to have seen a creature of massive proportions, dwarfing other objects on or near the water.

- Dark, Scaled Skin:

  The creature is often said to have dark, scaly skin, which glistens in the sunlight or moonlight. The coloration of Ogopogo's skin is typically described as being dark green, brown, or black, blending in with the murky depths of Okanagan Lake.

- Unusual Features:

  While the basic description of Ogopogo resembles that of a traditional sea serpent, some sightings include details of unusual features. These may include horse-like heads, large eyes, or other distinctive characteristics that set Ogopogo apart from known aquatic animals.

- Motion and Behavior:

  Witnesses often describe Ogopogo's movements as undulating or serpentine, with the creature gliding smoothly through the water or diving under the surface in a winding manner. Some suggest that Ogopogo exhibits behaviors such as breaching or splashing, though these sightings are less common.

- Duration and Detail:

  While some sightings of Ogopogo are fleeting and indistinct, others involve prolonged observations with detailed descriptions of the creature's appearance and behavior. Witnesses may provide sketches or diagrams to illustrate what they saw, adding to the credibility of their accounts.

- Variability in Sightings:

  Its important to note that descriptions of Ogopogo can vary widely from one sighting to another. Some witnesses report seeing a single large creature, while others describe multiple smaller creatures or a series of humps moving in the water. These variations in sightings contribute to the mystery and intrigue surrounding Ogopogo.

Descriptions and sightings of Ogopogo paint a picture of a mysterious and elusive creature that inhabits the depths of Okanagan Lake. While skeptics attribute many sightings to misidentifications or natural phenomena, the legend of Ogopogo continues to capture the imagination of those who seek to unravel the mysteries of this enigmatic lake monster.

From a scientific perspective, the existence of Ogopogo, the mysterious serpent, is highly contentious. While there have been numerous reported sightings and anecdotal accounts of the creature spanning decades, there is a lack of concrete scientific evidence to support its existence.

Here are some scientific perspectives on Ogopogo:

- Lack of Physical Evidence:

  Despite the numerous reported sightings and alleged encounters, there is no physical evidence such as remains, carcasses or biological samples that conclusively prove the existence of Ogopogo. Without tangible evidence to examine, scientists remain skeptical of the creature's existence.

- Natural Explanations:

  Many sightings of Ogopogo can be attributed to natural phenomena, such as floating logs, waves, currents or known aquatic animals. In some cases, eye witness accounts may be influenced by environmental conditions, optical illusions, or psychological factors, leading to misinterpretations or exaggerations of what was seen.

- Limited Habitat:

  Okanogan Lake, while large and deep, has been extensively studied by scientists, and its ecosystem is well-understood. The lake's conditions, including water temperature, depth, and nutrient levels, are not conducive to supporting large, unknown creatures like Ogopogo without leaving substantial ecological evidence of their presence.

- Cryptozoology and Pseudoscience:

  While some individuals may invoke cryptozoology, the study of creatures whose existence has not been sustained by mainstream science, as means of explaining Ogopogo, this field is often considered speculative and lacking in scientific rigor. Claims of undiscovered or mythical creatures often lack empirical evidence and are not taken seriously by the scientific community.

- Cultural and Psychological Factors:

  The legend of Ogopogo holds significant cultural and psychological significance for the people of Okanagan region and beyond. Belief in the creature may be influenced by cultural heritage, folklore, and a desire to preserve local traditions. Additionally, the human tendency to seek out mysteries and the unknown can contribute to the continuation of the Ogopogo legend.

- Research Efforts:
  Despite skepticism from the scientific community, some researchers have undertaken efforts to investigate the phenomenon of Ogopogo. These efforts have included sonar surveys of Okanagan Lake, underwater exploration, and attempts to capture photographic or video evidence of the creature. However, these investigations have thus far failed to provide conclusive proof of Ogopogo's existence.

While the legend of Ogopogo continues to fascinate and intrigue enthusiasts, scientists remain skeptical of its existence due to the lack of empirical evidence and the prevalence of natural explanations for reported sightings. Until conclusive evidence is presented, Ogopogo remains firmly entrenched in the realm of folklore and myth rather than established scientific fact.

Ogopogo, the mysterious serpent of Okanagan Lake, has become an iconic figure in popular culture, not only in Canada but internationally. Here are some examples of how Ogopogo has been featured in various forms of popular culture:

- Literature:

  Ogopogo has been featured in numerous books, both fiction and non-fiction. In fiction, authors have incorporated the legend of Ogopogo into mystery, adventure, and fantasy novels, adding an element of intrigue and suspense. Non-fiction books often explore the history, folklore, and scientific perspectives surrounding the creature.

- Film and Television:

  Ogopogo has made appearances in films, documentaries, and television shows. Documentaries exploring the legend of Ogopogo and other lake monsters have been produced, providing insights into the cultural significance of the creature and efforts to investigate its existence. Additionally, Ogopogo has been featured in fictional works, including animated series, where it serves as a plot device or source of inspiration for adventure stories.

- Art and Design:

  Ogopogo has inspired artists and designers to create various representations of the creature in paintings, sculptures, and other forms of visual art. These artistic interpretations often emphasize the serpentine form of Ogopogo and its mythical qualities, capturing the imagination of viewers and sparking curiosity about the legend.

- Tourism and Merchandise:

  The legend of Ogopogo has become a popular tourist attraction in the Okanagan region of British Columbia. Souvenirs, merchandise, and memorabilia featuring images of Ogopogo, such as T-shirts, keychains, and posters, are sold in local shops and gift stores. Businesses and attractions in the area may also adopt the name or image of Ogopogo to capitalize on its popularity with visitors.

- Music and Entertainment:

  Ogopogo has been referenced in songs, music videos and other forms of entertainment. Musicians may incorporate the legend of Ogopogo into their lyrics or album artwork, while filmmakers and animators may creature short films or animations featuring the creature. These creative expressions contribute to the ongoing fascination with Ogopogo and its place in popular culture.

- Social Media and Online Communities:

  The legend of Ogopogo has found a new audience on social media

  platforms and online communities. Enthusiasts and researchers share

  sightings, theories, and discussions about Ogopogo, fostering a sense

  of community and collaboration among those interested in the

  legend. Social media also serves as a platform for sharing photos,

  videos, and artwork inspired by Ogopogo.

Legends surrounding Ogopogo state that you may feel watched as you paddle out to Okanagan Lake, the mysterious creature known as Ogopogo watching from the depths of the shimmering water with deep hues of deep green and blue reflecting in the light.

Ogopogo, rarely seen, rises from the depths of the lake, its long body surfaces gracefully, the creature's skin glistening in the light, its scales reflecting an ambient glow. Ogopogo's head resembled a horse, rising above the surface, large eyes that scanned the surroundings with otherworldly intelligence.

Its movements smooth and serpentine, it seems curious about kayakers that may paddle close, Ogopogo circles around the small vessels with a sense of cautious curiosity. Meeting Ogopogo is not an ordinary encounter; it's a rare glimpse into the mysteries of the natural world that surrounds us.

To conclude, Ogopogo's presence in popular culture reflects its enduring appeal as a symbol of mystery, adventure, and the natural wonders of the Okanagan region. Whether viewed as a mythical creature of legend and lore or a real-life enigma waiting to be discovered, Ogopogo continues to capture the imagination of people around the world.

Introduction to Canada's Sasquatch: The Enigmatic Giant of the Wilderness

In the vast expanse of Canada's rugged wilderness, among the towering trees and misty mountains, roams a creature of legend and mystery. Known by many names across different cultures and folklore, it is famously known in Canada as the Sasquatch, this elusive giant has captured the imagination of Canadians and the world alike.

Sasquatch, also referred to as Bigfoot in other parts of North America, is a mysterious figure deeply rooted in the oral traditions of Indigenous people across Canada, including the Coast of Salish, Halkomelem, and Sts'ailes First Nations. Described as a towering, ape-like creature covered in dark fur, Sasquatch is said to inhabit the remote forests and mountainsides, leaving behind only elusive footprints and tantalizing glimpses to fuel speculation and intrigue.

In this introduction to Canada's Sasquatch, we embark on a journey into the heart of the country's wilderness to unravel myths, sightings, and cultural significance surrounding this legendary being. From ancient tales passed down through generations to modern-day encounters and scientific investigations, Sasquatch's story weaves a fascinating tapestry of folklore, mystery, and the enduring quest for answers.

Join us as we venture into the untamed wilderness of Canada, where the legend of Sasquatch awaits, beckoning us to explore the depths of its mysteries and contemplate the possibility that, amidst the vastness of nature, something truly extraordinary may yet be uncovered.

Sasquatch: Canada's Bigfoot Phenomenon

Sasquatch, often referred to Canada's Bigfoot, is a legendary creature that has been part of indigenous beliefs and North American folklore for centuries.

Here's a look at historical accounts and beliefs surrounding Sasquatch in Canada:

- Indigenous Traditions:

  Indigenous people across North America, including those in Canada, have long shared oral traditions and stories about hairy, ape-like creatures living in the wilderness. These creatures are known by various names in different languages, with sasquatch being one of the most used terms in English. Indigenous beliefs portray sasquatch as a spiritual being, often associated with the natural world and possessing supernatural powers.

- Historical Accounts:

  European explorers and settlers in North America documented encounters with large, hairy creatures resembling known accounts of Sasquatch as early as the 19th century. These accounts, often dismissed as folklore or tall takes, describe sightings of mysterious

creatures in remote wilderness areas, including the forests of Canada.
While some reports may be exaggerated or misidentified wildlife,
others provide detailed descriptions of humanoid figures that defy
conventional explanation.

- Cultural Resonance:

Sasquatch has become deeply ingrained in Canadian culture,
representing a blend of Indigenous traditions, folklore, and modern
popular culture. The legend of Sasquatch has inspired numerous
books, documentaries, films, and television shows exploring the
mystery and intrigue surrounding the creature. Sasquatch sightings
and encounters continue to be reported by people across Canada,
contributing to its lasting popularity and cultural resonance.

- Indigenous Perspectives:

Many Indigenous communities in Canada maintain beliefs and
traditions related to Sasquatch, viewing the creature as a guardian of
the wilderness or a spiritual entity with connections to the land. Some
Indigenous elders and knowledge keepers share stories and teachings
about Sasquatch as part of their cultural heritage, passing down

traditional knowledge and wisdom to younger generations.

- Environmental Conservation:

  Sasquatch lore also intersects with contemporary environmental conservation efforts in Canada. Some advocates argue that protecting Sasquatch habitats, such as old-growth forests and remote wilderness areas, is essential for preserving biodiversity and supporting healthy ecosystems. The legend of Sasquatch serves as a reminder of the importance of respecting and conserving the world around us.

In general, Sasquatch stands for a fascinating blend of Indigenous beliefs, historical accounts, and contemporary cultural phenomena in Canada. Whether viewed as a myth, cryptid, or a symbol of wilderness preservation, Sasquatch continues to captivate the imagination and spark curiosity among people of all backgrounds.

Physical descriptions and reported sightings of Canada's Sasquatch, often referred to as Bigfoot, vary widely due to the numerous encounters reported, leading many researchers to believe there could me "families" or whole different groups formed across the country.

Here are some common physical descriptions and examples of reported sightings:

- Height and Size:

  Sasquatch is typically described as a large, bipedal humanoid creature, standing anywhere from 7-10 feet tall, or even taller, depending on witness accounts – showing there may be multiple groups. Witnesses often emphasize the massive size and towering stature of the creature compared to humans.

- Hairy and Shaggy Appearance:

  Sasquatch is consistently described as being covered in dark or reddish-brown fur or hair, which appears thick, shaggy, and matted. The fur is said to cover most of its body, including its face, torso, arms, and legs.

- Narrowed Head and Pronounced Brow Ridge:

  Many witnesses also report seeing Sasquatch with conical-shaped head and a pronounced brow ridge, giving it a distinctly ape-like or primitive appearance. Some descriptions associate its facial features to those of a gorilla or ape.

- Muscular Build:

  Sasquatch is often described as having a robust and muscular build, with broad shoulders and a powerful physique. Sasquatch has been commonly observed as large, with muscular libs and chest, suggesting immense strength.

- Distinctive Features:
  While the overall appearance of Sasquatch is humanoid, witnesses often note certain distinctive features, such as its long swinging arms, large hands with opposable thumbs, and a wide, pungent odor emanating from the creature.

- Behaviour and Movements:
  Witnesses describe Sasquatch as moving with a smooth, fluid gait, covering large distances with surprising speed and agility despite its size. Some sightings include details of Sasquatch engaging behaviors such as foraging for food, vocalizing, or seeing humans from a distance.

- Location and Habitat:
  Reported sightings occur in diverse habitats across Canada, including remote forests, mountainous regions, and wilderness areas. Witnesses often encounter Sasquatch near bodies of water, such as lakes, rivers, and streams, where it may be seeking food or shelter.

- Variability in Descriptions:
  It is important to note that descriptions of Sasquatch can vary

significantly from one sighting to another, with differences in size, fur color, facial features, and behaviour. These variations may be influenced by environmental factors, lighting, condition, distance, altitude as well as individual perceptions of the sightings.

Reported sightings of Sasquatch in Canada tend to paint a picture of a mysterious and elusive creature that inhabits the remote wilderness areas of the country. While skeptics attribute many sightings to misidentifications or hoaxes, the persistence of eyewitness accounts continues to fuel public interest in the search for evidence of Sasquatch's existence.

Scientific investigations of Canada's Sasquatch, also known as Bigfoot, have been limited due to the lack of empirical evidence supporting its existence. However, there have been efforts to study reported sightings and claims from a scientific perspective, often with skepticism.

Here is an overview of scientific investigations and skepticism surrounding Sasquatch in Canada:

- Lack of Conclusive Evidence:

  Once of the primary reasons for scientific skepticism about sasquatch is the absence of conclusive physical evidence, such as remains (indicating they live an abnormally long time), DNA samples, or clear photographs or videos; despite numerous reported sightings and alleged encounters. So far, no definitive proof of Sasquatch's existence has been presented to date.

- Misidentification and Hoaxes:

  Skeptics continue to argue that many reported sightings can be attributed to misidentifications of known animals, such as bears, elk, or humans, otherwise misidentifications have been found to be hoaxes perpetuated for attention or profit. Without verifiable evidence to support eyewitness accounts, skeptics still are cautious in accepting Sasquatch as a legitimate scientific phenomenon or evolutionary species.

- Biological Implausibility:
Some scientists question the biological plausibility of a large, undiscovered primate species like Sasquatch inhabiting the remote wilderness areas of Canada. They tend to argue that such a creature would require a breeding population to sustain itself, leading to the accumulation of physical evidence such as nests, tracks, or fecal matter, which has not yet been found. This does not discount the existence of this species; however, it still is difficult to prove due to lack of evidence.

- Cryptid and Pseudoscientific Claims:
The study of Sasquatch falls within the realm of cryptozoology, which is often regarded as a pseudoscience due to its focus on investigating creatures whose existence has not been sustained by mainstream science. Claims of Sasquatch encounters may be dismissed by skeptics as anecdotal or speculative, lacking in scientific rigor.

- Skeptic Inquiry:
Despite skepticism, some researchers have approached the study of Sasquatch with open-minded inquiry, looking to investigate reported sightings using scientific methods and principles. These efforts may

include field surveys, data analysis, and collaboration with wildlife experts to evaluate the credibility of eyewitness accounts and search for liable corroborating evidence.

- Popular Culture and Mythology:
  Skeptics argue that the legend of Sasquatch has become deeply entrenched in popular culture and mythology, leading to a proliferation of exaggerated or fictionalized accounts that obscure scientific investigations. The cultural significance of Sasquatch may contribute to the perpetuation of the legend, making it difficult to separate fact from fiction.

Scientific investigations of Canada's Sasquatch remain inconclusive, with skepticism prevailing due to the lack of substantial physical evidence and the prevalence of alternative explanations for reported sightings. While some researchers continue to explore the phenomenon with scientific precision, skepticism persists among the broader scientific community until verifiable evidence of Sasquatch's existence is presented.

Sasquatch, also known as Bigfoot, has been a prominent figure in Canadian media and entertainment, captivating audiences with its mysterious and elusive nature.

Here are some ways Sasquatch has been featured in media and entertainment in Canada:

- Documentaries:

  Numerous documentaries have been produced exploring the legend of Sasquatch and investigating reported sightings and encounters. These documentaries often feature interviews with eyewitnesses, researchers, and experts in fields such an anthropology, wildlife biology, and cryptozoology. Canadian filmmakers have contributed to this genre, producing documentaries that focus on Sasquatch sightings in remote regions of Canada.

- Television Shows:

  Sasquatch has been featured in various television shows, both fictional and non-fictional. Some Canadian television series have dedicated episodes to exploring the legend of Sasquatch, delving into its cultural significance and the ongoing search for evidence of its existence. Additionally, reality TV programs have followed teams of Sasquatch enthusiasts as they conduct field investigations and search for clues in the wilderness.

- **Films:**

  Sasquatch remains the subject of numerous films, including both documentaries and fictional narratives. Canadian filmmakers have contributed to this genre by producing Sasquatch-themed films that explore the legend from different perspectives. These films may depict Sasquatch as a mysterious creature lurking in the wilderness or a misunderstood being struggling to survive in a hostile environment.

- **Literature:**

  Sasquatch has been a popular subject in Canadian literature, inspiring authors to write novels, short stories, and non-fiction books exploring the legend. These works of literature often dive into themes such as folklore, mythology, adventure, and the human fascination with the unknown. Canadian authors have added to the genre by incorporating elements of Canadian heritage, story telling and culture into these stories.

- **Art and Music:**

  Visual art is also one of the many forms used to capture the mystique and intrigue of the creature. Artistic representations of Sasquatch may include paintings, sculptures and illustrations that depict the creature in various settings and poses. Similarly, musicians may write songs or compose music inspired by the legend, exploring the themes of mystery, and exploration of the wild.

Even now, Sasquatch remains a compelling figure in Canadian media and entertainment, reflecting the country's rich cultural heritage. Whether portrayed as a fearsome monster, or gentle giant, Sasquatch continues to inspire creative expressions across various forms of media.

Legend has it that deep within the dense wilderness, hidden from prying eyes, lives a being unlike any other. Standing tall and mighty, with shaggy fur covering its immense frame, Sasquatch is a creature of myth and mystery.

In the heart of the night, when the moon hangs low and the forest is shrouded in darkness, Sasquatch appears from its hidden sanctuary. With silent steps, it roams through the ancient woods, its presence known only by the rustle of leaves and distant sound of branches snapping underfoot.

Those fortunate enough to catch a glimpse of Sasquatch speak of its towering stature and powerful presence. Its eyes, said to gleam with a wisdom beyond our understanding, peer out from the depths of the forest, watching, waiting as if guarding some ancient secret.

But Sasquatch is not a creature of malice; no, it is a gentle giant, a guardian of the wilderness, living in harmony with nature. It wanders the forests of Canada, its footsteps echoing through the ages, a reminder of the untamed beauty hidden.

Countless tales have been told of encounters with Sasquatch, whispered around campfires passed down through generations. Though some may dismiss these stories as mere fantasy, those who have felt the earth tremble beneath Sasquatches feet know the truth – they have glimpsed the magic that dwells within the heart of the wilderness.

So, as you venture into the great unknown, remember to tread lightly, and respect the land, for you never know what mysteries await in the depths of the forest. And who knows, one day you too will have the privilege of meeting the legendary Sasquatch, a creature of myth and legend, roaming the wilds of Canada for all eternity, long before us and long after.

Qallupilluit: Arctic Sea Creatures of Inuit Mythology

Introduction to Qallupilluit: Mysteries Beneath the Arctic Ice

In the icy realms of Canada's arctic, where the frigid waters meet the frozen expanse, lies a creature of legend that haunts the imaginations of Inuit children and elders alike. This creature, known as the Qallupilluit, is a chilling presence in folklore of the Indigenous people of the North.

The Qallupilluit is a mysterious being that prowl beneath the ice, waiting to snatch unsuspecting children or those who venture too close to the water's edge. Described as humanoid in appearance, with long, bony fingers and a face hidden beneath a hood or mask, the Qallupilluit embodied the fears and dangers of the Arctic environment.

In this introduction to the Qallupilluit, we embark on a journey into the heart of Inuit mythology and culture to uncover the secrets and significance of this elusive creature. From ancient stories passed down through generations to modern interpretations and artistic representations, the Qallupilluit's tale serves as a cautionary reminder of the dangers that lurk in the icy depths of the North.

Dive into the chilling waters of the Arctic with us where the legend of Qallupilluit awaits, ready to reveal the mysteries and wonders of Canada's northernmost reaches.

The Qallupilluit are mythical sea creatures from Inuit mythology primarily found in the folklore of the Inuit people of the Arctic regions of Canada, Greenland, and Alaska. These creatures are often malevolent beings that inhabit the cold, icy waters of the Arctic Ocean and other bodies of water in the region. Together we are going to take a closer look at Qallupilluit in folklore and mythology:

- Description:

  Qallupilluit are typically described as humanoid creatures with long, claw-like fingers and sharp teeth. They are said to have scaly, slippery skin that allows them to move swiftly through the water. Qallupilluit are often shown as being covered in seaweed or kelp, which helps them blend into their aquatic environment.

- Behavior:

  Qallupilluit are well known for their cunning and malicious intend, particularly towards children. According to Inuit folklore, they lurk beneath the surface of the water, waiting to snatch unsuspecting individuals, especially children who wander too close to the shoreline or venture out to the ice alone. Qallupilluit are said to drag their victims beneath the water to their underwater lairs, where they may be kept captive or eaten.

- Origins:

Origins of the Qallupilluit legend are rooted in the traditional beliefs and cultural practices of the Inuit people, who relied on storytelling to convey important lessons about survival, respect for nature and the dangers of the Arctic. Qallupilluit are believed to embody the dangers of the sea and the unpredictable nature of Arctic waters.

- Cultural Significance:

Qallupilluit hold significant importance to Inuit communities, where they are often invoked as a means of teaching children to respect the dancers of going out alone in addition to stay close to their families and communities for safety. The legend of the Qallupilluit also serves of a way to explain mysterious disappearances or accidents that may occur in this harsh environment.

- Survival skills:

Inuit elders and storytellers use the legend of the Qallupilluit to impart important survival skills and knowledge to younger generations, such as the importance of staying away from thin ice, avoiding dangerous areas of the shoreline, and always staying within sight of adults when near the water. By instilling a healthy fear of the

Qallupilluit, Inuit communities continue to protect their children from the dangers of the Arctic seas.

In Inuit mythology, the Qallupilluit are known mythical sea creatures primarily found the Arctic regions of Canada; these creatures are often depicted as malevolent beings that inhabit the icy waters and other bodies of water in the regions.

Here are some descriptions based on the Canadian Qallupilluit and their behavior based on Inuit folklore:

- Physical Description:

  The Qallupilluit are described as anthropological creatures with long, bony fingers tipped with sharp claws. They have a slippery, scaly skin that is often covered with seaweed or kelp, allowing them to blend in with most surroundings, the Qallupilluit also are believed to have gaping mouths filled with sharp rows of teeth, which they use to catch their unsuspecting prey.

- Habitat:

  Qallupilluit are often believed to inhabit the frigid waters of the Arctic Ocean, and other bodies of waters in the region, such as fjords, bays, and costal areas. They are often found in places where the sea of ice meets the ocean, Qallupilluit lurking beneath to ambush their victims.

- Known Behaviors:

Qallupilluit are well known for their cunning and predatory behavior

towards children and often target those who venture too close to the

waters edge. Children are the most common victims of the Qallupilluit

as they explore alone near the shorelines, on ice or out of the sight of

their loved ones. Qallupilluit have also been heard to mimic the voices

of loved ones calling out to them from the water.

- Abduction of Victims:

Once lured close enough, Qallupilluit will grab them with its long,

clawed fingers and drag them under the water to their lair. Some

accounts describe these lairs as caves or crevices hidden under the ice

or in the depths of the ocean. Once captured, victims may be kept

alive, or consumed as food.

- Precautions:

Inuit elders and parents warn their children to be cautious around

bodies of water and to avoid wandering too close to the shoreline or

onto thin ice, where the Qallupilluit are said to lay in wait. Children

are instructed to stay within sight of adults and to never approach the

water alone, especially in areas where Qallupilluit are believed to be

present. The legend of Qallupilluit allows parents and elders to use

these stories to instill a healthy fear in their children, reminding them to stay close to the safety of their communities and to avoid wandering too close to the water's edge.

Understandably, the Qallupilluit are feared and respected creatures in Inuit mythology, embodying the dangers of the Arctic waters and serving as figures in traditional stories and folklore warning of the possibilities of danger, making them cunning and formidable adversaries in the icy depths of the Canadian Arctic.

Additional cultural aspects surrounding the significance of the Qallupilluit, and beliefs include:

- Respect for Nature:

  The Qallupilluit embody the unpredictable and dangerous nature of the Arctic environment, reminding Inuit people of the importance of respecting and living in harmony with the natural world. The legend reinforces traditional beliefs about the interconnectedness of all living beings of the land and sea.

- Cultural Identity:

  An integral part of Inuit cultural identity and heritage representing the shared belief system and worldview that has been passed down through generations; the legend of the Qallupilluit connects Inuit people to their ancestors and to the land, reinforcing a sense of cultural continuity and resilience in the face of environmental challenges.

- Spiritual significance:

    In addition to their role in teaching survival practices, the Qallupilluit also hold significance in Inuit belief systems. They are seen as powerful and mysterious beings with supernatural abilities, capable of traversing between the physical and spiritual realms.

Overall, the Qallupilluit are creatures revered and feared throughout mythology, embodying important values and beliefs about the relationship between humans and the environment. Their legend will continue to be passed down through oral tradition, serving as a reminder of resourcefulness, resilience and spiritual connection to the land and sea of the Canadian Arctic.

In contemporary contexts, the legend of the Qallupilluit continues to resonate within many communities in Canada, serving as a cultural touchtone and source of storytelling tradition.
Here are some ways the Qallupilluit maintain relevance in contemporary contexts:

- Preservation:

  Within Inuit communities, efforts are made to preserve and pass down traditional stories and folklore, including those about the Qallupilluit. Elders and storytellers play a vital role in keeping these oral traditions alive, ensuring that younger generations stay connected to their cultural heritage and ancestral knowledge.

- Education and Awareness:

  The legend is often used as an education tool to teach the importance of safety and respect for nature. Lessons that derived from Qallupilluit stories emphasize practical skills for navigating the arctic environments, such as ice safety and understanding costal waters.

- Art and Expressions:

  The imagery of the Qallupilluit continues to inspire artists, writers, and filmmakers and persistently explores themes of environmental safety, cultural identity, environmental stewardship and the intersection of tradition and modernity.

- Environmental Conservation:
Inuit perspectives on the world as reflected in stories of the Qallupilluit, often prioritize environmental conservation and sustainability. Traditional knowledge about Arctic ecosystems and wildlife informs contemporary efforts to protect and manage resources in the face of climate change and other environmental challenges.

- Community resilience:
Resilience and resourcefulness embodies the stories of the Qallupilluit and resonate with communities facing social, economic, and environmental pressures. Drawing on cultural teachings, and values, community members work together to adapt and thrive in changing circumstances, drawing strength from their shared heritage.

- Cross-Cultural Understanding:
Outside of Inuit communities, the legend continues to influence the understanding and appreciation of Indigenous perspectives and worldviews. Through storytelling, art and cultural exchange, non-Indigenous audiences gain insight into traditions, aiming to foster

greater respect and collaboration across cultural boundaries.

The Qallupilluit are still relevant in today's context as symbols of resilience; by preserving and sharing these stories we can strengthen ties to their ancestral lands and traditions.

Legend has it that deep within the artic waters, where the icy currents swirl and the frozen winds howl, another creature lurks – a creature known as Qallupilluit. The Qallupilluit dwell beneath the frozen surface of the Arctic, their domain hidden from prying eyes of humans. With skin as cold as ice and scales shimmering like the northern lights, they glide through the frigid waters with an otherworldly grace.

Unlike Sasquatch, whose presence is felt among the towering trees of the forest, the Qallupilluit prefer the solitude of the icy depths below. They are elusive beings, rarely seen by human eyes, their legend lives on in the stories of those who walk the land.

Qallupilluit are not creatures to be trifled with, they are said to appear when the ice begins to thaw, their icy fingers reaching up to snatch away unsuspecting souls who dare venture too close to the water's edge.

However, despite their fearsome reputation, there are those who believe the Qallupilluit are simply misunderstood beings, guardians of the Arctic waters, watching over the delicate balance of life beneath the ice.

Loup Garou: Shape-shifting Werewolves of French-Canadian Folklore

In the depths of French-Canadian folklore, in the rugged landscapes and whispered tales of the wild, the fearsome creature known as the Loup Garou lurks. This enigmatic being, steeped in mystery and terror, is a cornerstone of the rich cultural tapestry of heritage weaving its way through the imaginations of minds everywhere.

The term "Loup Garou" finds its roots in French, translating to "werewolf" in English. Yet, unlike the lycanthropes of other traditions the Loup Garou has a distinct identity, blending elements of shape-shifting prowess a with the haunting presence of the untamed.

Legend has it that the Loup Garou prowls the dense forests and shadowy expanses of the Canadian landscape, often assuming the form of a wolf or hybrid creature, part human, part beast. Tales vary about the origin of these creatures, with some narratives suggesting curses inflicted upon individuals as punishment for transgressions against nature, while others speak of inherited afflictions passed down through bloodlines.

The transformation into a Loup Garou is said to occur during the full moon, a time when the boundaries between the human and spirit world blur, and primal instincts reign supreme. Those unfortunate souls afflicted with the curse are said to undergo a terrifying metamorphosis, their bodies contorting and twisting into the form of a monstrous world, driven by an insatiable hunger for flesh and blood.

Throughout history, the presence of the Loup Garou has instilled both fear and fascination among the inhabitants of Canada. Tales of encounters with these shape-shifting beings have been had down through oral traditions serving as reminders of dangers within the forests and the consequences of straying too far from the path.

Intriguingly, the legend of the Loup Garou continues to endue modern times, whether viewed as a symbol of primal wilderness or a harbinger of supernatural terror, the legacy of the Loup Garou remains an integral part of French-Canadian folklore; The origins of the Loup Garou are shrouded in the mists of time, blending elements of European werewolf lore with local cultural influences; its evolution a testament to the rich tapestry and mythmaking that has shapes the collective imagination.

Over time, the legend of the Loup Garou has evolved and adapted, while its origins may be rooted in folklore, its appeal continues to captivate the imagination, and inspire storytellers.

The Loup Garou, a prominent figure in French-Canadian folklore, is a creature of awe and dread, having a unique set of characteristics and behaviours that distinguish it from traditional werewolf lore.

Some key attributes of the Loup Garou are as follows:

- Shape-shifting Abilities:

  Central to the myth of the Loup Garou is its ability to shape-shift between human and wolf forms. Unlike traditional werewolves, whose transformations are often triggered by the full moon, the Loup Garou is believed to have more control over its shape-shifting abilities, able to assume its lupine form at will. This flexibility adds an extra layer of unpredictability and menace to the creature's nature.

- Hybrid Form:

  In addition to its human and wolf forms, the Loup Garou is often depicted as possessing a hybrid form, combining elements of both human and wolf anatomy. This amalgamation of features heightens the creature's otherworldly appearance, blurring the line between man and beast.

- Superhuman Strength and Speed:

  When in its wolf form, the Loup Garou is said to possess superhuman strength and speed, making it a formidable predator capable of outmatching even the most skilled hunters. Its uncanny agility and ferocity strike fear into the hearts of those who dare to venture into its domain.

- Predatory Nature:

The Loup Garou is portrayed as a relentless hunter, driven by an insatiable hunter for flesh and blood. It prowls the darkened forests and remote wilderness areas, stalking its prey with cunning and stealth. Victims of the Loup Garou are often torn apart with savage brutality, leaving behind grisly scenes of carnage.

- Curses and Afflictions:

In many legends, the transformation into a Loup Garou is depicted as the result of a curse or affliction, often brought about by transgressions against nature or encounters with malevolent forces. Individuals who fall victim to these curses are condemned to live as half-human, half-wolf, forever haunted by their primal instincts.

- Full Moon Association:

While Loup Garou is not always strictly tied to the lunar cycle like traditional werewolves, the full moon is often associated with heightened activity and transformations. It is during these lunar phases that the creature's powers are said to be at their peak, and encounters with the Loup Garou are most likely to occur.

- Fearsome Reputation"
Throughout French-Canadian folklore, the Loup Garou is feared and revered in equal measure. Its existence a reminder of the dangers lurking in the wilderness and consequences of straying too far from the path.

The Loup Garou embodies the untamed spirit of the wilderness, a creature of myth and legend whose presence continues to captivate and instill fear in the hearts of those who learn of the legend of the Loup Garou.

The cultural influence and beliefs surrounding the Loup Garou are deeply ingrained in Canadian legends and have left a lasting impact on traditions, storytelling, and societal values. Some key aspects of Loup Garou cultural influence and beliefs are as follows:

- Wilderness Symbolism:
  As a symbolic representation of the untamed wilderness the Loup Garou embodies the dangers that lie in wait. In French-Canadian folklore, the wild is often portrayed as a realm of mystery and peril, where the presence of the Loup Garou reinforces the idea that nature is both beautiful and terrifying, a place where primal instincts reign supreme. Despite its fearsome reputation, the Loup Garou is also associated with a deep connection to nature. In some interpretations this creature is a guardian of the forests and mountains, its duality reflecting the complex relationship between humans and the world around us; highlighting both reverence and appreciation inspired by the fear and unpredictability of nature.

- Morality and Punishment:
  The legend of the Loup Garou often contains moral lessons about the consequences of immoral or unethical actions. In many tales, individuals are cursed to become Loup Garou as punishment. This

emphasis on morality underscores the importance of living in harmony with one's surroundings and respecting balance.

- Indigenous Beliefs:
Indigenous people of North America had rich mythology surrounding shape-shifting creatures and spirits of the land. As Europeans settlers encountered and interacted with communities, cultural exchanged happened, resulting in the syncretism of myths and legends. This bleeding of cultural elements contributed to the unique character of the Loup Garou legend in Canadian legends.

- Identity and European Influences:
The originating roots of the Loup Garou legend can be traced back to medieval Europe, where tales of werewolves were prevalent in tales and mythology. These stories often showed people cursed to transform into wolves under influence of the full moon, taking themes of primal nature, fear of the unknown and the struggle between bestial instincts. French settlers brought these tales with them, where they merged with mythologies of the land as time went on.

- Environmental Factors:
  The harsh and untamed wilderness of Canada plays a significant role in shaping any legend, especially that of the Loup Garou. The vast forests, remote expanses, and rugged terrain fostered a sense of mystery and danger, providing fertile ground for proliferation of supernatural tales. The isolation and unpredictability of the environment further fueling imaginations as people sought to explain the complexities of life.

- Social and Psychological Dynamics:
  Beyond its origins in folklore and mythology, the legend of the Loup Garou also reflects deeper social and psychological dynamics within society. Themes of identity, community, and the struggle against base urges resonate throughout the legend, serving as allegories for the human condition and the perennial battle between civilization and wilderness, order, and chaos.

- Adaptation and Evolution:
  Over time, the legend of the Loup Garou has adapted and evolved to reflect changing cultural attitudes and societal dynamics. While ancient stories continue to be reinterpreted in literature, film, and other forms of media, it is reflecting contemporary concerns and

anxieties; this ongoing evolution ensures that the legacy of the Loup Garou remains relevant in modern times.

Loup Garou continues to captivate audiences across many forms of media including film, literature, video games and television. This reimagining often infuses traditional tales with new twists, themes, and settings, reflecting evolving cultural attitudes and storytelling techniques. Some examples of these modern interpretations of the Loup Garou are:

- Literature:

  Authors have often explored the legend of the Loup Garou through novels, short stories, and graphic novels. These works range from faithful retellings of traditional folklore to innovative reimagining that blend elements of terror, fantasy, and romance. Some authors delve into the psychological aspects of Lycanthropy, exploring themes of identity, transformation and the struggle between humanity and bestial instincts.

- Film and Television:

  The Loup Garou has been a recurring motif in film, appearing in a variety of genres ranging from horror to comedy. Filmmakers and showrunners often use the creature as a central antagonist or plot device, weaving it into a supernatural narrative that explore themes of survival, betrayal, and redemption. Modern adaptations may feature updated interpretations of the Loup Garou's appearance and abilities, utilizing state-of-the-art special effects to bring the creature to life on screen.

- Urban Fantasy:

In the realm of urban fantasy literature and media, the Loup Garou frequently makes appearance as part of larger supernatural worlds inhabited by vampires, witches, and other mythical creatures. These tales often reimagine the Loup Garou as a member of a secret society or hidden community, struggling to maintain a balance between their human and wolf natures while navigating the complexities of modern urban life.

- Video games:

The Loup Garou has also found its way into the world of video games, appearing as enemies, allies, or playable characters in various gaming titles. From action-packed adventures to immersive role-playing games. Video game developers draw on the rich mythology surrounding the Loup Garou to create compelling gameplay experiences that challenge players to confront their fears and assess their survival.

- Art and Illustration:

  Artists and illustrators often take inspiration from the legend of the
  Loup Garou to create visually striking works of art, ranging from
  detailed illustrations to stylized interpretations. These artistic
  representations may explore themes of revolution, primal energy, and
  the interplay between light and shadow, capturing the essence of the
  creature's enigmatic allure.

Legend has it that deep in the heart of the dense Canadian forests, where the trees stand as tall as the shadows grow long, there roams a living being of darkness and mystery- the Loup Garou.

Born from the whispers of the night and the howls of the wolves, the Loup Garou is a being of legend, feared by those who tread too far into the woods. With fur as black as the night sky and eyes that gleam with an unearthly light, it prowls through the darkness with a hunger that cannot be satisfied.

Some say that the Loup Garou is a cursed soul, condemned to wander the forests in search of its next victim. Others believe it to be a shapeshifter, taking on the form of a fearsome wolf to stalk its prey under the cover of darkness.

Regardless of the origins of the Loup Garou, one thing is certain – the Loup Garou strikes fear into the hearts of those who hear its name. Tales of its ferocity and bloodlust have passed through the generations, whispered around campfires, and recounted in hushed tones on winder nights.

And yet, among the fear and superstition, there are those who believe that Loup Garou is more than just a creature of darkness. They say it is a guardian of the forest, protecting its domain from those who seek to exploit its secrets for their own gain.

Memegwesi: Mischievous Spirits of Algonquian Mythology

In the rich tapestry of Algonquian mythology, amidst the whispers of the forests and the murmurs of flowing rivers, dwell the Memegwesi, unfathomable spirits drenched in mystery and mischief. These elusive beings, revered by some and feared by others, occupy a unique place in the tales of Indigenous peoples across North America.

The term "Memegwesi" originates from the Algonquian languages and refers to a diverse array of small, supernatural entities that are known to inhabit rivers, lakes, and forests. While descriptions of Memegwesi change among different Algonquian tribes, they are commonly depicted as diminutive humanoid figures with mischievous dispositions and magical abilities.

Despite their small stature, Memegwesi are acknowledged to possess great power and influence over their surroundings. They are often accompanied with the guardianship of waterways and the creatures that inhabit them, acting as protectors of fish, turtles, and other aquatic life. At the same time, however, Memegwesi are known for their capricious nature, delighting in playing pranks on humans who intrude on their areas.

Legends surrounding the Memegwesi are as varied as the land they inhabit. Some portray them as benevolent spirits who offer guidance and assist those who have shown them respect, while others depict them as tricksters who revel in causing chaos and confusion. In many stories, humans who encounter Memegwesi must navigate a delicate balance between appeasing these unpredictable spirits and avoiding their wrath.

The cultural significance of Memegwesi extends beyond their roles of mythical beings. They are deeply woven into the spiritual beliefs and practices of Algonquian people; rituals and offerings are often made to honor the Memegwesi and seek their favor, particularly when engaging in activities such as fishing, hunting, or traveling by water.

In contemporary times, the legends of the Memegwesi continue to resonate with many communities and others who wish to cherish the traditions of Algonquian mythology, their tales remind us of the importance of respecting the delicate balance of nature and honoring the spirits that dwell within. As guardians of the waterways and keepers of ancient wisdom, the Memegwesi serve as symbols of resilience, adaptability and the enduring bond of humanity and the earth.

The Memegwesi are mythical beings from the folklore of the Algonquian people of Canada, particularly among the Ojibwa, Cree, and Algonquin tribes. They are described as small, humanoid water spirits or trickster figures who inhabit rivers, lakes, and other bodies of water in the forests of Canada.

In many traditions and stories, the Memegwesi are believed to have supernatural powers and are associated with both beneficial and mischievous behavior. They are also known to play many tricks on humans especially when they are disrespectful. They are also Their attributes are as follows:

- Appearance:
  Memegwesi are commonly described as being very small in stature, often no taller than a child or smaller, they have humanoid appearances and human-like features such as arms, legs, and a head; with long hair and beards, usually unkempt, and sometimes possess shapeshifting abilities, invisibility, or other magical abilities. Some accounts also describe them as having wrinkled or weathered skin, reflecting their connection to the elements; they are said to live in hidden caves or under the water's surface, emerging only under certain conditions or to interact with humans.

- Clothing:
  Memegwesi are usually depicted as wearing traditional clothing or nothing at all. Their attire may be made from natural materials such as bark, leaves, or animal hides; in some stories or myths, they are

depicted as being naked or wearing only loincloths.

- Behavior:

Memegwesi are known for their mischievous and playful nature. They are tricksters who enjoy playing pranks on humans, especially those who intrude upon their territory or choose to disrespect nature. However, they can also be helpful and benevolent towards those who show them respect and reverence; often when you give them offerings, they will take that as a sign of peace, but be careful, it may also be a trick.

- Abilities:

Memegwesi are believed to possess powers, including the ability to control the waterways as well as manipulate the elements. They are said to have magical abilities like shapeshifting, invisibility, and the power to summon storms. Some stories attribute healing abilities to them as well, while others portray them as protectors of the wild and its inhabitants.

- Habitat:

Memegwesi are associated with remote and secluded areas of wilderness, particularly around bodies of water like waterfalls, lakes, and rivers; they have also been known to hide in caves, in underwater dwellings, or hollowed-out trees along the riverbanks.

- Cultural Significance:

Memegwesi play a significant tole in the traditions and storytelling of

the Algonquian people. They are often featured in myths, legends and

tales that are passed down from generation to generation. These

stories serve various purposes, including teaching lessons about

respect, consequences of greed or disrespect and the importance of

harmony with the natural world.

The Memegwesi are fascinating and complex figures in Algonquian folklore, representing a deep connection to the land and the spiritual beliefs of Indigenous people in Canada.

The Memegwesi play a significant role in both folklore and everyday life of the Algonquian people of Canada.

- Folklore and Mythology:

  In Algonquian folklore, the Memegwesi are prominent figures featured in myths, legends, and oral traditions passed down. They are central characters in stories thar explain natural phenomena, teach moral lessons, and preserve cultural beliefs. Memegwesi tales often revolve around themes such as greed, disrespect, respect for nature, and the importance of living in harmony; these stories serve as entertainment, education, and to reinforce cultural identity among Indigenous communities. These stories are looked to, to provide tales of sustainable living and treating the earth with care.

- Guardians:

  Also known as guardians, the Memegwesi are believed to protect the wilderness, particularly bound to water, as well as remote and secluded areas of the land, where they protect the environment and its inhabitants from harm. In this role, Memegwesi are revered and respected by people who seek their guidance and protection when navigating the wilderness.

- Everyday Life and Cultural Practices:

  While Memegwesi are mythical beings, they have a tangible presence in every day lives of Indigenous communities. References to Memegwesi can be found in various aspects of cultural practices, including art, music, dance, and ceremonies. Additionally, stories about Memegwesi are often shared during gatherings, festivals and other community events and heritage.

- Teaching Values and Ethics:

  Memegwesi tales continue to serve as educational tools for teaching values, ethics, and societal norms within many communities. Through these stories, Elders impart wisdom to younger generations, teaching them about respect, humility, cooperation, and reciprocity. Memegwesi stories also provide opportunities for intergenerational learning and the transmission of traditional knowledge from one generation to the next.

- Spiritual Revival:

  Many Indigenous revival movements also focus on revitalizing spiritual practices and beliefs that were disrupted by colonialism. The Memegwesi, as a spiritual being, deeply connects to the world, continuing to be invoked in rituals, prayers and ceremonies calling on them as guardians and guides. Their presence serves as reinforcement to the spiritual connection between the people and the land, fostering a sense of belonging and respect for traditional ways.

- Art and Expressions:
Many Indigenous artists and creators often draw inspiration from Memegwesi lore to produce visual art, music, literature, and other forms of expression that celebrate Indigenous culture and resistance. Memegwesi imagery can be found in paintings, sculptures, jewelry, and other artistic mediums, serving as powerful symbols of Indigenous identity and pride.

- Environmental Activism:
The Memegwesi association with the natural world also aligns with contemporary Indigenous environmental activism. As stewards of the land, Indigenous people continually advocate for the protection of natural resources, wildlife, habitats, and sacred sites, drawing on traditional teachings and beliefs embodied by figures like the Memegwesi. In this way, the Memegwesi become allies in the fight of

environmental justice and preservation of Indigenous lands and
cultures.

The Memegwesi presence in Indigenous revival movements, underscores their enduring significance as cultural symbols and spirit guides within the Algonquian traditions of Canada. Through storytelling, art, spirituality, and activism, the Memegwesi continue to inspire and empower Indigenous people in their ongoing struggle for cultural survival and self-determination.

The Memegwesi, also know as the Memegweshi or Mimi'gwasi, are mythological creatures from the folklore of various Indigenous people of North America, particularly among the Anishinaabe (Ojibwe) and Cree people. They are known as small beings often resembling little people or dwarves.

According to legend, the Memegwesi are benevolent beings, helping those who respect and honor the world, while causing trouble for those who harm it. These creatures protect the rivers, lakes, waterfalls, streams, and waterways; they are also said to have the ability to control the water, often associated with fighting and hunting. They are also well known for their craftmanship and are believed to have taught many people various skills, such as making traps and fishing nets.

In many stories, the Memegwesi are shy and elusive, only revealing themselves to those they consider worthy or to children. Overall, the Memegwesi are significant figures in mythology, standing for the importance of living in harmony and respecting the spirits that live in the world around us.

The exploration of cryptids in Canada reveals a fascinating tapestry of tales, myth and mystery woven into the fabric of the country's cultural heritage. From the dense forests of the Pacific Northwest to the icy waters of the Arctic, Canada's diverse landscapes provide fertile ground for stories of elusive creatures that have captured the imagination of many.

Throughout this exploration, we have encountered a diverse array of cryptids, each with its own unique characteristics and cultural significance. From the legendary Sasquatch, whose towering presence haunts the remote wilderness, to the enigmatic Ogopogo, said to lurk in the depths of Okanagan Lake, these cryptids embody the rich stories and beliefs passed down through Indigenous cultures and settler communities alike.

Skeptics may dismiss cryptids as mere legends or hoaxes, their enduring presence in Canadian folklore speaks to a deeper truth about the human experience. Whether as symbols of the untamed wilderness, guardians of the natural world, or reminders of the unknown prowling just beyond the edge of feeling, cryptids hold a special place in the collective consciousness of Canadians.

As we conclude our journey through the realm of Canadian cryptids, let us remember that the quest for these elusive creatures is not merely a search for physical evidence, but a celebration of the diversity of life, both seen and unseen, that inhabits this vase and wondrous land. Real, or imagined, cryptids remind us of the mystery and wonder that continue to shape our understanding of the world around us.